AMERICA'S
NATIONAL PARKS

First English edition published by Colour Library Books Ltd.
© 1984 Illustrations and text: Colour Library Books Ltd.,
    Guildford, Surrey, England.
This edition published by Crescent Books.
h g f e d c b a
Display and text filmsetting by Acesetters Ltd.,
    Richmond, Surrey, England.
Colour separations by Llovet, S.A., Barcelona, Spain.
Printed and bound in Barcelona, Spain by NECLOBE, and EUROBINDER.
ISBN 0 517 405520

AMERICA'S NATIONAL PARKS

Text by **CHRISTOPHER C. PICK**

Produced by
TED SMART and **DAVID GIBBON**

CRESCENT BOOKS
NEW YORK

CONTENTS

Man's traditional attitude – or rather, one should say, the traditional attitude of white, western man – towards the natural world has been one of superiority. Nature in all its manifestations is a resource to be exploited. Trees are felled for their timber; animals are hunted and shot for their skins and their meat; the seas are fished; the ground itself is torn up to gain the rich minerals hidden beneath. The list of depredations is endless. Nor is the damage and destruction merely short-term. Once destroyed, the balance of nature cannot restore itself in the next generation. Polluted rivers and streams stay polluted, and it is the work of decades to restore them to health. The scars across the land made by mining or quarrying take years to heal. And, above all, the delicately poised relationship of living things, the entire ecological balance, can easily be shattered by the exploitation of just one element within that balance.

This may seem a brutal characterization. But in essence it remains a true one. It can still be seen in the cynical and wholesale exploitation of the Amazonian rain forests and the destruction of indigenous communities there; in the proposed construction, now fortunately halted, of a dam in Tasmania on the site of an outstandingly important area for wildlife; in regular overfishing and the consequent destruction of fish stocks. It can be seen too, many people would argue, in the Superpowers' increasing emphasis on nuclear weaponry, which already forms a military arsenal that, should it be used, will destroy the natural, and the man-made world, once and for all.

The concept of a national park is in contradiction to the idea that man is at nature's disposal. National parks are founded in two beliefs: that people need substantial areas of the undisturbed, natural world in which to relax and recuperate; and that the natural world must be preserved on its own terms, for its own inherent values. Man's recreation, his literal re-creation; and the conservation of a world that far predates – and will far outlast – every manifestation of man. These two ideas, even though occasionally a little contradictory in practice, are the touchstones of the national park movement across the world. And it is indeed a matter for considerable optimism that in many nations – some 120 at the time of writing – the concept has taken root, has survived and thrives; the more so since in many of these countries very real, if short-term, economic advantage could be derived from exploitation of these areas.

It could be a matter of some surprise as well, that it was in the United States of America that the idea of a national park system originated. The USA is the land *par excellence* of individual endeavor. More than any other, the nation was created, its very physical boundaries set, by the efforts of many individuals rather than by a collective, centrally-directed impetus. Yet in many ways, the National Park concept is in total opposition to the ethic of the individual, for the National Park concept is founded, and remains almost entirely dependent, on government willingness to act in the common good and withhold land from exploitation.

We may now, with the benefit of hindsight, judge the American frontiersman harshly. The land was exploited for immediate economic gain, without any consideration at all for its long-term good management. Often long-established indigenous Indian communities were humiliated and cheated of their land, their way of life destroyed; and they themselves were expelled or killed. In the Great Smoky Mountains of Tennessee, for instance, the Cherokees could present little resistance to the first European settlers, and in 1828, having lost their land and culture, they were marched off to alien Oklahoma, and much of their land was cleared for agriculture. The start of the 20th century saw the land invaded a second time – by timber companies which, in little more than two decades, stripped the centuries-old forests, felling two-thirds of the trees. Mill towns were built, streams dammed and then released to carry away logs: once fertile soil became a wasteland, prey to fire and erosion.

This is one example of man's rapaciousness. Another is in the sequoia forests of California. Here, in barely forty years – at the end of the nineteenth century – loggers wiped out virtually an entire forest, including many of its finest specimens – trees more than a thousand years old. On a smaller scale, this happened countless times as the frontier was pushed to its westernmost limits.

Yet at the same time, two counter-influences were developing, and these eventually came together to lessen the frontier's rawness. One was literary – found chiefly among east-coast writers and artists. The other originated among some of the early settlers themselves.

Early proponents of the idea of a national park system included George Catlin, who spent much of the 1830s studying the Indians of the far west. In 1841, he produced a two-volume work entitled, *Manners of the North American Indians*. Others were the botanist William Bartram and the celebrated ornithologist John James Audubon. Writers such as James Fenimore Cooper, Ralph Waldo Emerson and Henry David Thoreau, all found spiritual refreshment in nature at its most wild, and strongly criticized contemporary, utilitarian values which looked to the land only for economic gain. For them, the survival of wildernesses was a matter of great psychological importance for a land whose character had been so profoundly marked and defined by the very existence of untamed land. This idea took root, and by the 1860s the first practical handbook on conservation, *Man and Nature*, by George Perkins Marsh, had been published.

By no means were all frontier settlers insensitive men, impelled by financial motives alone. The very beauty and isolation of the frontier drew many men to it. They found in the landscape a quality that touched their souls. Such men included the writer and naturalist Enos Mills, who travelled west to the Rocky Mountains in 1884, at the age of fourteen, and devoted many years of his life to campaigning for a national park in the Rocky Mountains. His aim was fulfilled in 1915, when the Rocky Mountain National Park was established. Another celebrated pioneer of the national park movement was John Muir – Scottish born, Wisconsin raised – whose love for the Sierra Nevada led him to press for, and eventually obtain, state and federal protection for the region. Of the threat to the redwoods and giant sequoias of California he once wrote dismissively: 'No doubt these trees would make good lumber after passing through a sawmill, just as George Washington after passing through the hands of a French cook would have made good food.'

Without the efforts of such people, the first national parks would never have been established. Huge tracts of wilderness, their wildlife and vegetation, would have been lost to the plow, the axe, the miner's shovel – and the nation would have been much the poorer. We owe them a great deal.

In 1870, scarcely more than a century ago, the Yellowstone region of Wyoming and Montana was barely known. A few trappers and prospectors had explored it, but the stories they brought back of its spouting geysers and amazing scenery were dismissed as fanciful travellers' tales. That year, under the leadership of General Henry D. Washburn, surveyor-general of the Montana Territory, an expedition set out to explore the area. What its members saw confirmed those earlier accounts – confirmed them not merely as the truth but, if anything, as over-modest reports of the splendors of the land. Discussions in camp brought forth the idea, thought to have originated from Cornelius Hedges, a Montana judge, that the region should be preserved as a national park for the benefit of the people. A two-year campaign followed, in the Press and in Congress, and in 1872 the world's first national park – the Yellowstone National Park – was established.

Yellowstone was not quite the first region to be set aside for the public's benefit. Eight years earlier, a small part of the Yosemite Valley in California had been similarly dedicated. But the reserve here was tiny; there already existed a flourishing tourist trade and, in any case, control rested with the state authorities, not with the federal government. This area later became part of the much larger Yosemite National Park, which was established in 1890.

Now that it had taken root, the National Park concept quickly spread – both within the USA and elsewhere. Setting up its first national park in 1887 – near Banff, Alberta –

Canada simply used the wording of the Yellowstone Act. In the USA, four more parks were founded in the 1890s – Yosemite, Sequoia, Mount Rainier and General Grant (now known as Kings Canyon). By the time the National Parks Service was formed in 1916, there were sixteen national parks and twenty-one national monuments. Smaller than national parks, national monuments are intended to conserve a single natural feature.

But this is to look some way ahead. In the intervening years some major battles had to be fought. One of the first was in Yellowstone itself. A sceptical Congress had gone along with the idea of a national park, at least partly because it had been convinced that no economic use for the land could be found: there were, after all, frosts in every month of the year. But by 1886, valuable mineral deposits had been located underground, and a proposal was made to build railroad tracks across the Park. The issue went to Congress, very much on the lines of the interests of free enterprise and commerce versus the national heritage – and the national heritage won: permission was refused. Two decades later, equal fortune did not attend the argument over Hetch Hetchy; a narrow valley in the Yosemite National Park. San Francisco needed water and proposed to flood the valley, which John Muir considered the equal in beauty of the Yosemite Valley further south. And the San Francisco authorities eventually won.

Setback though this undoubtedly was (John Muir died of a broken heart), it led directly to the National Park Services Act of 1916, which strengthened and safeguarded the status of National Park territory. Since then the Service has gone from strength to strength and, more importantly, the conservationist philosophy behind it has gained increasing acceptance. However, not total acceptance: in the mid-1950s, a battle was necessary to save the Dinosaur National Monument from being submerged by a dam. A few years later, Glen Canyon, which although one of the finest canyons in the nation, but not a protected area, was lost underneath the waters of Lake Powell. And in the mid-1960s, a veritable storm of public protest greeted an astounding proposal to construct two dams in the Grand Canyon itself, the very symbol of the USA's splendid landscape. In 1968, the developers eventually had to admit defeat.

The problems that the National Park movement has faced in the last decade are subtler than those of sheer survival, but crucial none the less. The legislation establishing Yellowstone stated that the region was to be 'set apart as a public park or pleasuring-ground for the benefit and enjoyment of the people'. The Act that set up the National Parks Service was worded in similar, though not identical terms: 'to conserve the scenery and natural and historic objects and the wildlife therein and to provide...for the enjoyment of the same...by such means as will leave them unimpaired for the enjoyment of future generations'. While numbers of visitors remained relatively low, these two functions – conservation and public recreation – remained, by and large, compatible. But recent years have brought more and more visitors to the National Parks. The most popular park in 1982, Great Smoky Mountains, had well over eight million visitors; and that same year, the ten most popular had between them no less than 30 million. Such numbers, welcome though they of course are in many respects, bring many difficulties with them, and the national park administrators have had to develop skills of management and control. To preserve the environment, the number of visitors to parts of many parks, are strictly limited. Some areas are designated wilderness areas, which remain strictly undeveloped. Camping permits, and permits issued to backcountry hikers, are rationed; the number of cars entering a park is severely limited, and visitors are encouraged to take to their feet.

The number of visitors is an outward sign of the conflict – sometimes potential, sometimes actual – between recreation and conservation. But, in fact, it goes far deeper. For some decades after 1916, the Parks' first priority was tourism. Hotels were built within Park boundaries; stores, shops and golf courses encouraged; roads constructed. Even the Parks' most precious resources – their wildlife and vegetation – were enlisted as entertainment. In Yellowstone, bears were fed garbage and grandstands were erected for visitors to watch. Spotlights played over 'Old Faithful' in the same Park. In Yosemite, a fire of logs and bark was pushed every night off Glacier Point – 3,000 feet above the Yosemite Valley.

But slowly attitudes began to change. A biocentrist approach came to predominate – an approach that values the natural landscape and its wildlife for itself, above all else, and one that gives first priority to the preservation of the wild environment on its own terms. Visitors must accept the land as it is. Few concessions are made to their comfort and convenience.

This is surely as it should be. The time scale of the natural world is far, far greater than that of any individual human being. The landscapes of our National Parks were being formed millions – often hundreds of millions – of years ago. And the geological changes that are taking place before our very eyes – but so imperceptibly that we cannot observe them – will continue for millions of years to come. Our role, as visitors to the magnificent National Parks of the USA, in all their diverse majesty, is that of the humble outsider. With the right attitudes, we can observe, we can learn, we can participate in the natural environment, more than we ever think we can. We can, indeed, re-create ourselves and return to our normal lives – our jobs, our schoolwork, our mundane day-to-day concerns and anxieties – refreshed and conscious of a greater splendor, a greater glory, in our land.

ACADIA

Acadia National Park preserves a little of the justly celebrated Maine shoreline for the nation – preserves it undeveloped, subject only to the relentless force of the sea and the elements. The ocean crashes in remorselessly – slowly undercutting the cliffs, gradually building up the tiny beaches. It brings fogs, too – fogs that can descend suddenly and without warning, blanketing the landscape, muffling all noise, so that the familiar becomes strange and alien.

The land itself has been shaped by ice – by huge glaciers that only 70,000 years ago covered the area. Ice scooped out the lakes on Mount Desert Island. Somes Sound, which nearly bisects the island, is a glacial lake drowned as the ice melted and the sea rose. Ice rounded the mountain tops and left behind huge boulders, stranded as the ice retreated.

The Park has three parts: the southern tip of Schoodic Peninsula, including Little Mosse Island; Mount Desert Island; and, some way to the south-west, Isle au Haut. Mount Desert was named by the French navigator Samuel de Champlain, who ran aground there in 1604 as he was exploring the New England coast. Isle au Haut was named by him, too. For years the area was under French influence; the English only settled there after 1760. Shipbuilding and fishing were for long the major occupations here, and commercial fishing remains important – especially for lobsters, sardines, scallops and crabs, and further offshore, cod. Today, tourism is a major business.

However, within the Park, the priority remains the natural world: the forest and mountains behind the sea; sea birds and seals; the sea itself, with starfish and sea urchins; and the fascinating world of the seashore, its tide-pools washed twice daily by the tides and brimming with marine life.

ARCHES

The very names arouse the visitor's anticipation: Upper Fiery Furnace, Devil's Garden, Parade of the Elephants, Garden of Eden, North Window. Contorted into strange and elaborate shapes, these huge rock formations stretch across the Utah red-rock country, north from the old pioneer Mormon settlement of Moab. Here, in a hostile and unyielding land, there are not far short of a hundred towers, spires, pinnacles, windows, arches, passageways, coves, and rocks balanced one on the other, all formed by the passage of time and the unceasing impact of the elements.

The geological process began some 150 million years ago. The wind deposited a 300-foot layer of sand, now known as the Entrada Sandstone. Buried by further deposits, the Entrada Sandstone gradually hardened into rock. Later, exposed once more as the result of erosion, a lengthy process of weathering began – and still continues today. Cracks in the sandstone grew larger, forming narrow canyons. Loose sand was swept away by wind and water. The softer stone in many of the narrow walls, or fins, separating the canyons, wore away more rapidly, producing the perforations, needles and delicate silhouettes the visitor sees today.

This is a secret, at first sight deserted, land where the human visitor feels dwarfed by nature's remote and lonely grandeur. But there is some wildlife. At night, deer, coyote and foxes may appear; and in the day there are rodents, small reptiles, rabbits and birds. The sparse vegetation is chiefly piñon and juniper, but in early summer the moist places can be carpeted with a profusion of wild flowers.

BADLANDS

It was with good reason that the indigenous Indians called this area *mako sica* (bad land). The French-Canadian trappers who crossed the region in the early-19th century, some of the first white men ever seen here, reported in similar fashion. *Les mauvaises terres à traverser* (bad lands to cross), was their description. And something of the same atmosphere strikes the contemporary visitor. There is an eerie, hot stillness here, seemingly lifeless, almost as if one were on the moon. Bad lands, indeed.

But it was not always so. Twenty-five to thirty million years ago there was teeming animal life here. Camels and three-toed horses (both no bigger than medium-sized dogs); sabre-toothed cats; titanotheres (rhinoceros-like creatures) and tiny oreodonets – all roamed a wide, swampy plain fed by rivers from the hills to the north. Their skeletons vanished into the ooze, or were buried by sediment – and are visible now in the countless thousands of fossils that dot this area. On the fossil trail, many are preserved under plexiglass on the exact spot where they were discovered.

The intervening millennia brought much geological activity. First, layers of volcanic ash from the west were deposited; visible still as the whitish sand that covers the Badlands. Gradually, the rain ceased and dry winds came from the north; the mammals died, and prairie grasslands replaced the marshes. Rivers continued to flow – but now they cut into the soft land, creating spectacular shapes. Animal life has returned – prairie dogs, coyote, badger, bison, porcupine, chipmunks, snakes, jack rabbits, cottontails and pronghorn.

The bison are a reminder that change is not wrought by nature alone. As recently as the early-19th century, there were huge herds of bison in this prairie country. In 1839, one such herd was estimated to cover no less than 1,350 square miles. You did not – you could not – count individual bison. You measured the herd instead. For the Plains Indians, the bison were essential to life – providers of meat, clothing, shelter and tools. But the bison were doomed. The frontier was pushing rapidly westward. For the settlers, anxious to have a stake in economic prosperity, these animals were an unprofitable encumbrance. The land was needed for crops. The bison were exterminated, and by 1889 scarcely a thousand survived. Now the patient work of the National Parks Service has brought them back to their natural habitat.

BIG BEND

For a little more than two-thirds of its course, from the San Juan mountains of Colorado to the Gulf of Mexico, the mighty Rio Grande river forms the border between the United States of America and Mexico. From El Paso, the threefold junction of Mexico and the states of Texas and New Mexico, the river flows south-east to the Big Bend. Here, amid the sheer walls of a series of grand and rugged canyons, it turns abruptly north-east, before slowly falling towards the ocean again.

It is around this Big Bend that one of the nation's most majestic National Parks is situated. The land is desert, part of the Chihuahuan Desert that covers much of northern Mexico and southern Texas. Its arid soil bears cacti and a surprising variety of scrub-like vegetation: in spring, from February through May, the desert does indeed bloom. And from the desert rise up the Chisos Mountains, tall and gaunt (7,835 feet at Emory Peak, the highest in the range), and almost ghostly. The word *Chisos* is said to signify 'ghost' or 'spirit'.

And it is down through the rocky heights of the Chisos that the Rio Grande has carved its way, during countless centuries. In its canyons – the Santa Elena, the Mariscal and the Boquillas – man is dwarfed by towering slabs of rock and can have but one sensation – that of submissive awe.

The canyons are best visited by boat. But skill and experience are required to handle a craft in tricky waters, especially in spring when they become full floods. For those not absolutely confident, the land-trails that lead into Santa Elena and Boquillas Canyons are preferable. Elsewhere in the Park there are ample opportunities for hiking and horse-riding, and for identifying the abundant plants and wildlife.

BRYCE CANYON

Set water to work on the land – water in the form of streams and rain, snow and ice – for millions of years, and the results can be spectacular. Bryce Canyon is evidence of this. Hundreds of tiny streams slowly cut down into the land, creating a series of overlapping semicircular bowls, or amphitheatres. Where there were faults and fissures, the water exploited them, leaving huge slabs of rockface exposed. Water worked on these too, dissolving and cutting away the softer rock, forming gullies and creating the weird and magnificent shapes and formations – spires, needles, towers, arches – we see today.

The Pink Cliffs from which Bryce Canyon is formed are relatively young: no more than 50 to 60 million years old. They are the most youthful part of a geological 'Grand Staircase'; a sequence of cliffs stretching south to the northern rim of the Grand Canyon and dating back more than 225 million years.

The Pink Cliffs are well named. For here, it is not only the shapes of the rocks that fascinate and enthrall, but their colors as well. Iron oxides, manganese and copper in varying combinations create the multitude of different shades: the more manganese, the more lavender and green; the more iron, the more pink and red.

For the visitor, the National Park is doubly attractive. There is spectacle, certainly, in the cliffs themselves. And there are the subtler, but no less genuine pleasures of the forest and meadows, and their extensive wildlife: well over 160 species of birds, coyote, badger, and many other night hunters: mule deer, porcupine and even a few cougar, elk and black bear.

And the name Bryce? It recalls Ebenezer Bryce, a Mormon settler of Scottish descent who tried to scratch a living here from the land. His only surviving comment on his home for five years is: 'A hell of a place to lose a cow!' The Paiute Indians were more lyrical, and just as accurate. Translated, their name reads: 'Red rocks standing like men in a bowl-shaped canyon'.

CAPITOL REEF

This National Park takes its name from a reef, a ridge of rock that acts as a barrier, said to resemble the Capitol – the domed building in the nation's capital that houses Congress. But the Park's principal and most fascinating feature is the Waterpocket Fold: a dramatic and geologically unique fold of rock more than 100 miles long. The name came about because of the pools of water that collect in the rock after rainstorms, attracting creatures such as shrimps and spacefoot toad tadpoles.

The Fold forms the southern part of the Park; a remote, spectacular area where visitors can hike in undisturbed solitude. The single road is normally passable by passenger automobiles, but care is needed. The fertile valley of the Fremont River lies at the center, and to the north is the confusingly named South Desert, another isolated region crossed only by creeks and dirt roads that deteriorate rapidly in flash floods. Here, too, hiking and horseback-riding are the best means of travel. Everywhere there are grand rock formations – arches, towers, pinnacles, canyons, monoliths.

Past inhabitants settled, naturally enough, along the banks of the river, and the first of these, to our knowledge, were the Fremont Indians around AD 800. Their stone tools have been found, and the moki huts (storage bins) they built of wood and rock to preserve corn, beans and other crops, can still be seen. The Fremont left about 1200 – why is uncertain, but a severe drought may have been the reason – and until about 1880 there was no permanent settlement, although Paiute Indians did hunt there. Then the Mormons sowed crops, planted orchards (the name of their settlement was Fruita) and established a few limekilns. There was even some uranium-mining. But the land could not support a thriving community, and by the late 1960s the last inhabitants were leaving. Now, however, the National Park, designated in 1971, has brought new purpose to the land.

CANYONLANDS

Two rivers – the Colorado and its tributary the Green – lie at the heart of the Canyonlands National Park. Over millions of years their force – individual at first, from the north-west and north-east, and then collective after they meet – has carved out over 100 miles of canyons, many half a mile deep. Of these, Cataract Canyon is perhaps the best known and most dramatic. For many visitors, the highlight of their vacation is an organized float trip down the Green or the Colorado and then through the Canyon. But this is just one of many hundreds of rock formations brought about by the unremitting action of water: by the rivers themselves, or by underground water eroding the 3,000-foot thick layers of salt that lie underground, causing sandstone slowly to subside into the space once filled by salt and forming long, narrow canyons, called grabens. Erosion works at varying speeds, softer rocks being attacked more easily and quickly than harder ones. The consequence is a fantastic collection of shapes that no human sculptor could imitate.

This is a desert land, with much wildlife. But for man, it is an untamed and relatively unexplored country. There is some evidence of past settlement, however. The Anasazi lived here for some thousand years, hunting and farming, making pottery and baskets. Their pictographs and petroglyphs, left on rock walls throughout Canyonlands, provide some record of their existence.

CARLSBAD CAVERNS

By rights, this should be two National Parks, not one. Above ground, in the Guadalupe Mountains, there is fine, rugged, hiking country, with dramatic canyons, high ridges and a magnificent abundance of wildlife: more than 600 species of plants, over 200 of birds, and many mammals, including raccoon, gopher, skunk, mule deer, bobcat, mountain lion and elk.

But it is below ground that the real wonders are to be found. The descent into the earth takes the visitor more than 800 feet into a series of majestic, awe-inspiring and immense caves: no less that 67 of them, the largest almost 1 mile long and 350 feet high. This is a geological wonder of the world: spectacular rock formations, iridescent stalagmites and stalactites etched with vivid colors and twisted into every imaginable shape. Devil's Spring, American Eagle, Frozen Waterfall, Frustrated Lovers, Queen's Chamber and Queen's Draperies, Hall of the Giants, Temple of the Sun – the very names suggest their grandeur.

It is simple rainwater that has created these galleries – rainwater trickling slowly down during hundreds of millions of years, imperceptibly (so imperceptibly that not even the longest-lived person would notice any change) dissolving the limestone rock.

And then there are the bats. Hundreds of thousands of bats live here – nobody knows the exact number; there are simply too many to count. From late spring to early fall, every evening at sunset, they stream out of the cavern entrance in a vast moving column that from far-off appears like a huge plume of smoke. Five thousand are said to leave every minute in search of their insect food and the exodus can take several hours. At sunrise they return, ready to sleep the day through.

CHANNEL ISLANDS

The Channel Islands are a scattered group of eight islands off the southern coast of California. Of the eight, three –

Anacapa, Santa Barbara and San Miguel – are open to visitors; a further two, Santa Cruz and Santa Rosa, while still remaining in private ownership, fall, nevertheless, within the boundaries of the National Park.

Reaching the islands can be tricky. The surrounding sea is frequently rough; both the ocean and the wind can rise rapidly, and fog can descend swiftly and without warning. Visitors arriving in their own boats need adequate tackle and the appropriate maritime charts, plus some sailing experience. But commercial boat trips are also available.

Once safely anchored, however, you find yourself in a whole new world – a timeless one into which technology and the priorities of mainland life cannot intrude. There are all the activities you would expect: fishing, swimming, scuba diving, hiking, camping. But even these will pall beside the majesty of an island sunset, or watching a pack of sea lions swimming lazily through the water just offshore, or hearing the gentle lap of tiny waves breaking on the rocks, or observing a solitary seagull circle in an azure-blue sky. On all three islands there is the grotesque-looking tree sunflower, or giant coreopsis, which grows up to 10 feet high is some protected spots, as well as a wealth of other vegetation. There are fascinating tidepools to explore, where the marine life is successively submerged in water and exposed to the air in a twice-daily cycle. There are birds to spot – black oystercatchers, cormorants, guillemots, auklets, snowy plovers and many more, including brown pelicans, whose only large west-coast nesting site is on Anacapa. And then there are the sea mammals: several species of seal and sea lion are resident; and between January and March, migrating groups of gray whale pass near Anacapa.

CRATER LAKE

Misnomer though it is, the name Crater Lake, nevertheless, tells you exactly what to expect: a lake lying not in a volcanic crater, for a crater may yet erupt, but in a huge caldera, or bowl, created by the collapse and death of a volcano.

The collapse happened circa 5,000 BC – in geological time the equivalent of yesterday. For half a million years the massive 12,000-foot Mount Mazama had erupted periodically, throwing out magma from its core. Eventually the cone became so weak internally that the magma chamber emptied, and the mountain literally vanished, scattering ash over more than 5,000 square miles in an explosion whose force was more than forty-two times greater than those at Mount St Helens in 1980. Where there had been a mountain peak there was now a large, empty, burning hot caldera. Volcanic activity continued for some while, sealing the caldera and throwing up Wizard Island, a symmetrical cinder cone.

Eventually, once the caldera had cooled sufficiently, water began to collect, deepening and widening the lake. Today, its depth (at a maximum of 1,932 feet the deepest in the USA and the sixth deepest in the world) varies by no more than 3 feet a year, evaporation and seepage almost exactly balancing the contribution of rain, snow and springs. Crater Lake is a closed ecological system, since no stream runs in or out, and the three fish species found there have all been introduced by man.

What its name cannot warn the visitor to expect is the sheer beauty of Crater Lake. The Lake itself is a deep and vivid blue, offset in winter by the snow that lies thick all around (on the highest peaks it remains from October to July). Surrounding the Lake are the rolling mountains, volcanic peaks and evergreen forests of the Cascades range – a truly spectacular setting for a truly spectacular work of nature.

DENALI

Denali – The High One – is the apt and simple name the Indians of Alaska gave this towering, 20,320-foot giant, its twin peaks rising high and straight. Mount McKinley, the European name for the mountain, and the name by which the National Park of which it is the dramatic centerpiece was known from its establishment in 1917 until 1980, was bestowed by a gold prospector, William A. Dickey. His reason – no doubt appropriate then, but almost laughably inappropriate now – was that William McKinley, of whose nomination for President Dickey heard on his return from the wilderness, was a fellow-supporter of the gold standard.

Within this immense and lonely wilderness, man has no place. Even the hardiest and most persistent hikers must consider themselves but brief visitors, poised on the edge of an unwelcoming world. But while man cannot adapt, there is plentiful bird and animal life – no less than 37 mammal and 155 bird species. There are caribou, moving in herds of several thousand along ancient migration routes; moose; Dall sheep, which migrate in summer too, to the high mountain crags; reindeer; elk; bison; bear and wolves. There are beaver, red squirrels, singing voles, snowshoe hares and, among the birds, golden eagles, arctic tern and warbler, golden plover and ptarmigan.

In summer, the thin top layer of the subarctic tundra melts, and enough plant life grows to support the wildlife population. Beneath, there are deep beds of permafrost – land frozen for thousands of years and drier than many deserts. High up in the mountains, although below the permanent snow line, the dry tundra supports dwarf rhododendron, forget-me-nots and a wealth of other tiny plants. Lower, in the moist tundra, there is cottongrass, sedge and dwarf shrubs, including willow and birch. In the *taiga*, strips of land that follow the rivers, white and black spruce grow, along with paper birch, balsam, poplar and quaking aspen.

But winter is a different world. Most birds escape by migrating to more southerly and equable climes. The animal population survives the arctic temperatures by hibernating (ground squirrel), sleeping (grizzly bear), or subsisting on concealed food stocks (beaver, red squirrel). A few of the animals, such as snowshoe hare and ptarmigan, take on a white coat and struggle to survive in a hostile environment.

EVERGLADES

The word Everglades means a marshy land covered with tall grasses – a 'river of grass'. And a river of grass exactly describes this unique place, the largest remaining subtropical wilderness in the USA. The entire area (less than half the Everglades itself falls within the boundaries of the National Park) is a shallow, slightly tilted bowl, lined with limestone and edged with a limestone rim. Through this bowl the freshwater of Lake Okeechobee, to the north of Everglades, moves gradually, virtually imperceptibly, towards the ocean. Over thousands of years this river of grass – 6 inches deep and 50 miles across – has developed and maintained its own ecosystem, containing a rare blend of tropical and temperate species.

It was this unique environment that the National Park was established, in 1934, to preserve and protect. Much damage had already been done. The outlying areas had been built over. Hunters had virtually wiped out many species: herons and snowy and great egrets, for instance, had been pursued almost to extinction for their plumage. Land had been drained for agricultural use, and the drainage channels had both brought poisonous salt water in, killing many plants, and had dried many areas out, leaving them vulnerable to fire.

The Park still faces problems, chiefly competing demands for scarce water supplies, and its ecosystem remains delicately balanced. But, for the moment, Everglades is a precious sanctuary for many endangered species. Here you may see alligators and, on the saltwater rim, crocodiles; the manatee or sea cow; the cougar or Florida panther; great white herons and southern bald eagles; green sea turtle; peregrine falcon. These, and many other species, find respite here from man's continuing depredations.

The characteristic Everglades view is of a green and brown expanse of sawgrass, a tooth-edged sedge that grows nearly

10 feet high. The view is broken by hammocks, islands of trees and jungle poised on outcrops of limestone a few feet above the surrounding marsh. Here there are tangled thickets of palms, gumbo limbo and mahogany trees, ferns and orchids, all growing hugger-mugger. On the coast itself, there are mangrove wildernesses and stretches of coastal prairie, where cactus, agave and yucca plants grow.

GLACIER

The Waterton/Glacier International Peace Park is a unique national park, a symbol of co-operation and understanding between the nations. That the two nations concerned – the USA and Canada – are old and staunch friends and allies, is less important than the symbolism of the decision made in 1932 by the Canadian Parliament and the US Congress to merge their respective national parks. It was a recognition that the natural landscape and the creatures and vegetation that inhabit it are world assets, not purely national ones. The lesson, half a century on, still needs to be recalled.

And what a landscape it is, with hundreds of miles of towering snowcapped peaks, spectacular canyons, rushing waterfalls, ice-blue lakes and deepgreen forests. This is glacier country. No less than four times in the last three million years, thick sheets of ice have covered it, sculpting the land as we see it today, creating peaks and passes, ridges and valleys. But before that – at least sixty million years before, perhaps more – the land itself had been shaped in a massive series of upheavals. Ancient rocks, originally on the ocean floor, thrust themselves up, and a huge slab of rock was propelled about 50 miles eastwards over the existing and much younger mountain range.

There are three distinct climates here. On the western side of the Park the climate is Pacific – warm and moist, with fir, pine, spruce and larch forests. In the east, prairie conditions prevail, with red and white geraniums, asters, Indian paintbrush and other characteristic flora. In the Alpine areas, the wild flowers are at their most magnificent – gentian, glacier lily, heather. And here, too, there is a wide variety of wildlife, often easily visible from the many hundreds of miles of trail in the back country: bighorn sheep, black bear, mountain goat, moose, wapiti.

GRAND CANYON

Words genuinely fail – the language is too poor in adjectives to do justice to the wonder of the Grand Canyon. Even the plain statistics – 277 miles long measured along the river,

between 600 feet and 18 miles wide, and about a mile deep – cannot truly convey the atmosphere of this most celebrated and most impressive of all the United States' many natural beauties. The photographs help. From them the reader can begin to appreciate the Canyon's stunning grandeur; its ever-changing light and colors. But it is perhaps only on an extended visit, when there is time to observe and explore, that one can see into the Canyon's heart, and come to terms a little with this amazing work of nature.

It is the river that has created this spectacle; the swift-flowing Colorado that some 25 million years ago began to scour the flat plateau, cutting through layer after layer of rock. The scouring continues, as it has done for eons, at the rate of about 6½ inches every thousand years. This entire area is ancient: the first rocks were formed some 1,700 million years ago, when mountains were thrust up, only to be almost entirely eroded again. The rocks of these first mountains can be seen at the foot of the Inner Gorge, where the Colorado now runs. Another upheaval produced more mountains, and these again were almost entirely eroded. Rocks from this era form the second layer of basement rocks in the gorge. Some 550 million years ago the canyon area became a basin, collecting over the next 300 million years, layers of sandstone, shale and limestone that form the upper parts of the canyon walls. Finally, only 65 million years ago, the earth's crust started to rise; snow and rain from the Rockies began to search for a way to the sea, and the Colorado River started to establish its course.

The descent into the Canyon is thus a journey into our geological past, each of the multicolored layers representing a different era, down to some of the oldest rocks known on earth. It is also a journey through numerous climatic zones: in fact the Canyon has six of the northern hemisphere's seven life zones. This has fascinating consequences for the animal life of the area. The north and south rims of the Canyon may not be many miles apart, but for many species the gap is unbridgeable: to cross it would mean passing through life zones with unsuitable climate and food. Thus, the Abert and Kaibab squirrels. Their habits are very similar, and before the Canyon was formed they surely had a common ancestor. But now the Abert lives south of the Canyon, the Kaibab north, each remaining isolated from the other.

GRAND TETON

Like so much else on this continent of stunning natural beauty, the Grand Teton range was formed as a result of cataclysmic geological upheaval. In common with the Sierra Nevada, the Grand Tetons are fault-block mountains: a steep escarpment rising sheer out of the plain on the eastern side, with gently sloping foothills to the west. What happened, many millions of years ago, was that pressures in the earth's crust transformed what had been the seabed into mountains. Still greater pressures made the rocks break into two parts along a fault. The western half was tilted up and over the eastern half, creating the western foothills and the steep eastern face. The newly uplifted mountains forced the clouds from over the Pacific higher, increasing rainfall on the west side of the mountains. The streams swelled, and those flowing east, which now had less far to go, carved out deeper canyons, carrying debris onto the plain. Glaciers continued the process, deepening the canyons and scouring out glacial lakes.

These, then, are the geological events. The result is a spectacular mountain range. The three stars in a firmament of majesty are the three highest peaks, named *Les Trois Tetons* by an early French traveller: Grand, Middle and South; 13,770, 12,798 and 12,505 feet high respectively. Accompanying them are deep-green forests, brilliant glaciers, steep canyons, ice-blue lakes and streams. Here dwell undisturbed: elk, moose, black and grizzly bear, bighorn sheep, beaver, weasel, coyote, and many other animals.

One natural curiosity deserves mention. The Continental Divide – the watershed between east and west – runs through the National Park. Water falling on one side eventually reaches the Atlantic, while on the other side it makes its way to the Pacific. High in the Tetons lies Two Ocean Pass, a tiny lake with two outlets. One, Atlantic Creek, pursues its course to the Gulf of Mexico via the Missouri and the Mississippi; while the other, Pacific Creek, flows to the Pacific by way of the Columbia River.

GREAT SMOKY MOUNTAINS

The statistics concerning this National Park are quite simply fantastic. Within its half million acres there are over 1,400 different kinds of flowering plants; 350 species of mosses and related plants; about 2,000 species of fungi and some 130 kinds of tree. The tulip trees reach nearly 200 feet into the air, chestnut oaks 100 feet. Nearly 250 bird species have been seen in the mountains, and some 50 mammal, 40 reptile and 70 fish species dwell here. Three-quarters of the Park is wilderness: there are 700 miles of streams, 800 of trails and sixteen peaks over 6,000 feet – the tallest, Clingmans Dome, is 6,643 feet high. The land itself is old – 400 million years old, which is three times as ancient as the Rocky Mountains.

But probably the most remarkable fact about the Park is not another item in a long list of statistics. It is the very fact of the

area's survival. For thousands of years after man first walked the earth, the Great Smoky Mountains lay undisturbed, barely marked by human intervention. The change came in the early-19th century, when European settlers arrived. The forests vanished, as did the indigenous Cherokees, and agriculture, logging and mining all but ruined the land forever.

That this seems barely credible now, is a tribute to the successful conservation policies practised in the Park over the last half-century. Some 40 per cent of the original forest – the forest that the Cherokees knew – remains: a moist, misty and deeply wooded world of coves, waterfalls, tumbling streams and balds, that might never have been threatened. Balds are an interesting phenomenon of the Great Smoky Mountains. There is no treeline in the Park, and the highest peaks are thickly wooded. Balds are smaller peaks, yet treeless and with a cover of grass and sedge, or heaths such as rhododendron or laurel.

Some eight million visitors come here each year. The Park absorbs them all, offering each individual the opportunity for real physical and mental re-creation.

GUADALUPE MOUNTAINS

A barrier reef in Texas, much like the celebrated reef off the coast of Queensland, Australia, seems a paradox. But such a reef is at the heart of the Guadalupe Mountains National Park. About 280 to 225 million years ago a large, shallow, salty inland sea covered some 10,000 square miles of what is now Texas and New Mexico. A reef was built-up of lime-secreting algae and other organisms; a lagoon formed between the reef and the land; the lagoon was gradually filled in, and the reef was buried. For the most part it has remained that way, deep beneath the hot, lifeless Texas plain. But in a few spots it is exposed, most notably on the eastern escarpment of the Guadalupe mountains, in the Carlsbad Caverns National Park and, on the Texas side of the state line, in the Guadalupe Mountains National Park.

For the geologically-minded visitor, the spot to make for is McKittrick Canyon, in whose 1,900-foot north wall there is a remarkable cross-section that includes the core of the reef itself, plus fore-reef and back-reef deposits.

This single feature, reminder of a Texan landscape very different from the present one, should not lead us to ignore the many other diverse environmental features of this National Park. There are no less than four separate climatic zones, varying between those prevailing in southern Canada and in northern Mexico; and three ecological zones, between the lowest point in the Park, 3,650 feet above sea level, and the tip of Guadalupe Peak, 8,749 feet up. There is both desert and high-country vegetation; a rarely found association. The abundant wildlife – more than 200 species of bird, and 52 of reptiles and amphibians have been recorded – is likewise unusually mixed. This is the northernmost limit for many Mexican species, and the southern and easternmost for many species from the Rocky Mountains.

HALEAKALA

Two quite distinct areas make up this National Park on the Hawaiian island of Maui. There is the crater of Mount Haleakala which has given its name to the Park – a strikingly bizarre landscape that seems to belong to the moon rather than to our own planet. And, in startling contrast, there is Kipahulu – a region of pools, cascades and waterfalls, pastoral valleys and grasslands, rain forests and rugged coastal cliffs.

Like all the Hawaiian islands, Maui is the product of millions of years of undersea volcanic eruptions. Originally there were two separate volcanoes, whose summits slowly climbed from the seabed and eventually emerged above the waves. The island was formed when they were joined by an isthmus created by lava, alluvium and ash. Haleakala is the larger of these volcanoes (it stands some 12,000 feet above sea level and about 30,000 feet above the ocean bed). The crater is, in fact, misnamed. It is the result, not of volcanic activity, but of prolonged erosion during a time, many millions of years ago, when the volcano was dormant. Since then, however, multicolored symmetrical cones up to 600 feet high have been formed from ash, cinders and spatter blown out of vents within the crater.

Now, Haleakala (the name means House of the Sun) is quiet once more. There were two minor lava flows at a low level in 1790, and earthquake records show that all is not yet settled deep within the mountain. But it is now almost certain that it will never erupt again.

On its eastern edge, the Park gives protection to the fragile ecosystem of the Kipahulu area. Native birds survive here still (in many other parts of the island chain, species imported by white settlers have virtually obliterated the native species), as does a large tract of the koa and 'ohi'a rain forest, still almost undisturbed by civilization. Here, too, there are bamboo, mango, guava and kukui, and the 'Ohe'o stream, normally placid, occasionally torrential, joining the numerous sparkling pools.

HAWAII VOLCANOES

The Hawaiian islands are simply a chain of volcanic mountains. Over many millions of years molten rock, or magma, has forced its way from deep in the earth up through the ocean bed. The magma slowly forms enormous undersea mountains, mountains so large that some eventually emerge through the waves as islands. Many of the volcanoes thus formed are now extinct: the turmoil way beneath their summits is stilled, and the lava no longer flows. The reason why, is because the island chain is moving – slowly, almost imperceptibly – some 2 to 3 inches a year northwest, but moving nevertheless. The Hawaiian islands are positioned on a section of the earth's crust known as the Pacific Plate, and it is this plate that is on the move, cutting the volcanoes off from their source of magma.

Of all the Hawaiian islands, Hawaii itself is the largest. Its three greatest volcanoes are Mauna Kea, Mauna Loa and Kilauea, and the last two of these make the centerpiece – the stars indeed – of the Hawaiian Volcanoes National Park. And great they are: Mauna Kea and Mauna Loa are claimed to be the greatest mountain masses on the planet, measured from the ocean floor. Mauna Kea rises 15,000 feet before it breaks the waves, and then continues a further 13,796 feet; Mauna Loa is almost as high, and Kilauea only some 5,000 feet shorter.

Nor are these volcanoes extinct. Mauna Loa and Kilauea are among the most active anywhere on the planet. Kilauea erupts almost every year, pushing lava from its summit and from rifts in its side, in spectacular displays. On a number of trails that cross the Park, molten lava lies beneath the crater surfaces. Most spectacular of all is Mauna Ulu, or 'Growing Mountain', a new parasitic lava shield on the east side of Kilauea, from which huge amounts of lava have poured.

This National Park is a vivid reminder that nature is not still; that geological forces remain at work.

HOT SPRINGS

This is a most unusual National Park. Its heart is not an awesome stretch of landscape, or an outstanding environmental feature, but a far smaller and more modest manifestation of nature: a series of hot, therapeutic springs bubbling out of the ground. It is also far older than any other National Park, having been set aside as a reservation as early as 1832, well before Europeans had even set foot in many of the areas described elsewhere in this book.

But its history long predates that. For centuries before the first white man came (the Spanish explorer Hernando de Soto in 1541), native Americans had gathered here on neutral ground; a place to which members of any peoples could come in perfect safety. The USA acquired the springs in 1803 as part of the Louisiana Purchase from France, along with a vast stretch of territory in what are now the southern states. And almost immediately visitors were arriving to take the waters. Soon the federal government went into partnership with private interests, developing bathhouses and ensuring the water supply. In this century, the 1920s and late-1940s have been boom periods – and although numbers of visitors have declined of late, the resort flourishes still.

What, then, is it that attracts seekers of health and relaxation? As at other spas, it is the quality of the waters. Here the thermal water is naturally sterile: no bacteria whatsoever are present. It gushes from the ground at a constant temperature – 143 degrees Fahrenheit – and contains traces of a number of valuable minerals: calcium, magnesium, bicarbonate and fluoride among them. Steam cabinets, whirlpools, massages, alcohol rubs, hot and cold packs, and many other treatments, enable visitors to obtain full benefit and refreshment from the waters.

And these waters may be a remarkable age. The water that gushes forth from the springs today, started as rainwater that was absorbed deep into the earth through fractures and cracks in the rock. Heated by contact with hot rocks, it then returned slowly to the surface, in a cycle that can occupy as long as 4,000 years.

ISLE ROYALE

Isle Royale is a rare phenomenon in the late-20th century. It is a natural habitat, some would say a true wilderness – the only one in the USA, outside Alaska, that remains scarcely disturbed by man. There were once trading posts here, and beaver-trappers and copper-miners came. But they have long since gone and nature has once more reasserted herself.

Here there is genuine isolation. The devices of civilization hardly intrude: there is no public telephone system, for instance. The island's sense of remoteness is enhanced by its physical position in the middle of Lake Superior – 15 miles from the nearest shore, and a three to six hour boat journey away from the mainland ports. Even in the height of summer, bad weather and rough water can delay or postpone the voyage.

When you arrive, you will find a world of dense vegetation and forests, lakes, streams and offshore islands. The best way to explore is by boat or on foot. There are 160 miles of foot trails, one of the most spectacular running along the Greenstone Ridge – the island's central backbone. There is fishing too, and an amazing variety of aquatic environments: streams, rivers, warm-water ponds and the waters of Lake Superior itself.

The story of two of the most interesting species on the island is fascinating. Moose reached Isle Royale by swimming there sometime early this century. By the 1930s, there were so many that food stocks could not cope, and the moose began to die. A fire in 1936 made matters worse, and numbers fell sharply, only to increase yet again as fodder grew once more. But in the winter of 1948-9, a pack of wolves crossed the ice from Canada, established itself on the island, and now the two species, prey and predator, together create a natural balance: the wolves culling the weak and old moose, thus maintaining a healthy population.

LASSEN VOLCANIC

30 May, 1914: quite unexpectedly, without any warning signs, Mount Lassen breaks some two centuries of inactivity and erupts, sending a stream of molten lava downhill. The crater, on the north slope near the summit, is quite small at first, only 45 feet wide, but within two weeks it grows to 1,500 feet in diameter. Ash and steam reach a height of three miles. Almost a year of quiet follows. Then, on the night of 19 May, 1915, there is another explosion, far more devastating than before. Molten lava rushes down Lost Creek and Hat Creek; the steam released with it melts the snow and a horrendous, tumultuous mud slide, at times 18 feet deep, destroys everything in its path. A few days later, yet another explosion of steam and hot ash wipes out whatever has managed to survive. The land is stripped clean, and some five million feet of timber are lost.

Mount Lassen is quiet now. Visitors can enjoy the serene beauty of the National Park – the lakes (there are more than fifty); the deep green forests; the flower-filled valleys. They can follow the 150 miles of foot trails, and look for the birds and animals that make their home here.

But reminders of nature's might remain. Bumpass Hell (named for a man who fell into a mudpot in 1865 – and survived) is a seething area of hot springs, mudpots and fumaroles. The Devastated Area still remains denuded of vegetation, nearly seventy years after the explosion that overwhelmed it. The Hot Rock – a huge boulder of lava – lies where it came to rest in 1915. Its name comes from the fact that it remained hot for days.

Until 1980, one could write of Lassen that it was the only volcano on the US mainland to have erupted this century. But the dramatic explosion of Mount St Helens, 400 miles to the north in the same volcanic range, reminds us that inside, Lassen remains in turmoil. The events of 1914 and 1915 could repeat themselves.

MAMMOTH CAVE

There are 150 miles of explored passageways in this subterranean complex, and many times that length remain unexplored. The names the early speleologists gave the caverns, rooms and passages, are a vivid demonstration of their awe at what they found: Frozen Niagara, Grand Central Station, Rock of Gibraltar, Rocky Mountains, Old Bull's Concert Hall. It is an impressive, solitary world underground: long passages stretching and disappearing into the distance, large multicolored stalactites, weird shapes chiselled out of the rock.

This is a limestone cave. Its story started millions of years ago under the sea, when the skeletons of tiny marine animals collected and solidified to form limestone. Later, after earth movements had brought the limestone onto dry land, a slow attack by water began. Exploiting all the cracks and crevices, the water gradually seeped through – dissolving the limestone, its sediments also scouring out chambers. The final chapter was a fall in water level underground, which left us with the network of caves we enjoy today.

There is much to do above ground, too, in this National Park. There are trails through the beautiful hardwood forests, some leading to springs that emerge from the caves beneath the walkers' feet. There is the forest wildlife to observe. And there is the Green River, which runs through the Park, to enjoy.

MESA VERDE

Mesa Verde means 'green table', and the name must date from sometime in the middle of the 18th century, when the first Spanish explorers reached the area. But, although they had been unoccupied for several hundred years, the mesas – high plateaus dotted with spruce, juniper and piñon, and cut through by deep canyons – had been the site of a flourishing and elaborate Indian civilization. The evidence preserved for us to marvel at today, consists chiefly of groups of dwellings large enough to house an entire community and built in caves on the cliff face. These are elaborate shelters: the Spruce Tree House, for example, has eight ceremonial chambers and no less than 114 living rooms.

Little is known of the cliff-dwellers. They seem to have moved down from the mesas into their precarious cavern dwellings towards the end of the 12th century. Why is uncertain. One reason may have been fear of attack: the open mesa was vulnerable to assault, the enclosed canyon far more secure. Whatever the reasons, they must have been good ones, for life can hardly have been congenial there: extrèmes of heat in summer and cold in winter, and a long climb up to the fields on the mesas. Within a century, the cliff-dwellers had vanished entirely, driven out, it is now thought, by prolonged droughts and bad harvests at the end of the 13th century.

Before the move to the cliffs, the mesa tops had been occupied for some six centuries, first by people known as Basket Makers, because of the elaborate examples of their skills they left behind. They lived in pithouses dug in the ground. Their successors were Pueblo Indians who dwelt first in houses made of poles, sticks and mud, and later, during the 12th century, in sturdy, sizeable stone-built houses, some of which had as many as three stories and fifty rooms.

For us today, fascinating examples of many of these different dwellings remain, together with an enthralling collection of everyday objects, once discarded and abandoned but now preserved for our interest and enjoyment.

MOUNT RAINIER

A jagged, eternally-snowcapped peak rises high in the distance, and dominates the land around for many miles. Beneath it lies a dense green enclosing forest, and fields and valleys of wild flowers in gorgeous display. Small wonder then, that Mount Rainier exerts such a pull, for it is for many a place of re-creation.

At 14,410 feet, Mount Rainier – or Takhoma, to give it its Indian name – is not quite the highest peak on mainland USA, but many claim that it is the most striking. It is, in fact, a dormant volcano, though not necessarily a dead one. On the summit there are two craters, and although there has been no major eruption for two thousand years, and no minor one since 1870, steam still rises from the craters' edges, melting the icecap a little and creating steam caves. On occasions these have been lifesavers, when climbers trapped by bad weather have found refuge in them.

No less than twenty-seven named glaciers surround the summit – an expanse of ice covering some 35 square miles, slowly moving downhill, still shaping and reshaping the mountain. In warm weather, an avalanche of ice, snow and rock may suddenly break off from a glacier and hurtle downwards; or mud and rock trapped beneath the ice may work free and slide down in an unstoppable mudflow.

Below the snowline, the subalpine meadowland – home of deer, mountain goats and marmots – is vibrant and full of color. Wild flowers abound in astonishing numbers: no less than 700 different species have been counted. Each year, spring bursts into life at successively higher levels as the snow melts, and suddenly there is blossom everywhere and carpets of blooms beneath one's feet. So tightly packed are the forests further down the slopes – Pacific silver firs between 3,000 and 5,000 feet; Douglas fir, big-leaf maple, red cedars, western hemlock below 3,000 feet – that the sun can scarcely penetrate, and the valley floors are draped with moss and ferns.

NORTH CASCADES

This spectacular National Park at the northern end of the Cascades range in northern Washington state, contains some splendidly wild and isolated country. Much of the land is virtually unexplored, and is accessible only to experienced backcountry hikers willing to take to the cross-country mountain trails. Those who do so, find a stimulating and challenging world of glaciers and crevasses, cliffs, spires and pinnacles, snowfields, high peaks and tumbling waterfalls. There are meadows full of Alpine flowers, and forests of western red cedars and Douglas firs.

These are relatively young mountains: a volcanic range whose present shape was etched during the (geologically) recent ice ages, which carved their steep slopes, deep valleys and jagged ridges. Remnants of the ice ages are found in the many glaciers in the Park – no less than 318, which is more than half of all the glaciers in the USA's lower 48 states. The glaciers are formed when moisture-bearing clouds, coming in from the Pacific, are forced upwards on the western side of the Park. Their moisture falls as snow which, since the rate of melt is lower than the snowfall, compacts into ice.

The North Cascades National Park is part of a rather larger recreation area. The Park itself is split into two units, northern and southern, divided by the Ross Lake National Recreation Area. Here, there are three dams built between 1924 and 1949 on the Skagit River to provide electricity for Seattle. And at the south-eastern tip of the National Park lies the Lake Chelan National Recreation Area; a magnificent wilderness in the Stehekin Valley. Lake Chelan, resting in a glacial trough, is among the nation's deepest lakes: its bed is 1,500 feet down, some 400 feet below sea level. Stehekin itself, an isolated community at the head of the lake, can be reached only by foot, boat or plane. But it is a trip well worth the effort.

OLYMPIC

Within the 900,000 acres of the Olympic National Park lies a fascinating variety of wilderness: rain forests, Alpine meadows, snowcapped peaks, crystal streams and rivers, and a long and rugged stretch of Pacific coastline. It is an untouched land – virtually as pure as the day when white men first came here. Settlement started in the mid-19th century, with fur-trapping and timber-cutting along the coast. But the interior remained unknown until 1890, when a party of five explorers set out to discover its wonders. Returning awed at what they had seen, they proposed a national park. Twenty years later their suggestion became reality, and a substantial area, later extended, came under federal protection.

It is the Pacific Ocean, crashing relentlessly onto the Park's 50-mile shore, that creates the Park's environment. Wind and clouds gusting in from the west rise as they cross the coast and reach the mountains, shedding their water on the peaks. Mount Olympus, at 7,965 feet the grand centerpiece of the Park, is the wettest place in the continental United States, receiving some 200 inches of rain every year. From the peaks the water falls rapidly, often as meltwater from glaciers, becoming first a rapid stream and then a rushing river. At 1,000 feet the rain forests begin: a dense, green jungle of trees, moss, shrubs, fallen trunks and branches, in places quite impenetrable.

Above the rain forest lies a belt of temperate forest; above that, mountain and subalpine forest; and finally, over 5,000 feet, the Alpine zone is reached – a merciless tundra in which only arctic plants, mosses and lichens can survive. On the shore, of course, there is yet another – quite different – environment, with sea stacks, cliffs and tidepools.

The wildlife is as varied as the environment. Deer, marmot, black bear and Roosevelt elk (safe now from the hunter's gun) can all be seen. Along the coast there are raccoons and harbor seals, sometimes even migrating gray whales.

As an area of natural, unspoilt landscape, Olympic National Park is unsurpassed. Come here to hike, climb, fish or ride. But, above all, come here to learn from the natural world. You will not be disappointed.

PETRIFIED FOREST

'Painted Desert and its trees turned to stone' was the way US

Army surveyors and mappers described this area when they first crossed it in the 19th century.

The trees 'turned to stone' are indeed just that. Once, perhaps some 200 million years ago, trees did grow here. Floods felled them, burying them in marshy land. Ground water containing large quantities of silica and other minerals gradually seeped through the wood, dissolving its fibres. In its place were substituted exact copies of the trees, including their rings and cells, but in minerals, not in wood. Finally, after numerous geological upheavals, erosion set to work, slowly removing the shales and sandstones – sometimes as much as 3,000 feet deep – that covered the petrified trees, leaving them exposed and scattered across the land.

These trees, some as large as 100 feet long and 8 feet in diameter, bear an uncanny resemblance to genuine trees. Their very brilliance, their vivid colors and their crystal-like patterns, made them the object of rapacious collection, and many thousand tons were removed before the area became a national park. Today, severe penalties are imposed on anyone attempting to remove even the tiniest piece.

The 'Painted Desert' of that early description, takes its name from the minerals and impurities the rocks contain. Iron compounds produce an endless variety of subtly different shades of red and brown; organic material results in dark greys and black. Weathering is important too: brilliance and freshness of color also depend on how long a layer of rock has been exposed to the weather.

Those first explorers failed to mention a third feature of the area, now carefully preserved since the National Park was established – there has been human habitation here for over 2,000 years, as the ruins of Indian villages, potsherds and petroglyphs bear witness.

REDWOOD

The Redwood National Park preserves the celebrated coast redwoods of northern California. By no means all of them, however, since nearly two million trees originally grew here before westward expansion brought the frontier settlers in the 1820s and 1830s. Today, barely half – perhaps far fewer – still survive. The problem has been that the coast redwood makes excellent lumber, unlike the giant sequoias of the Sierra Nevada. Redwood neither shrinks nor decays; it is straight-grained and easy to work. With qualities like these, and with the ever-increasing demand for manufactured goods of all kinds during the last and present centuries, how could the redwoods resist the advance of the loggers? It was only after many years' effort, with persistent resistance from lumber concerns, that some protection was won – and even now logging continues outside the boundaries of the National Park.

Among the trees that will be conserved, however, is the tallest in the world: a 367.8-foot specimen discovered on the banks of Redwood Creek in 1964. Coast redwoods are also among the oldest trees in the world (though not the oldest, as that honor goes to the giant sequoias), some specimens living 2,200 years.

Once, millions of years ago, when dinosaurs inhabited our planet, and the climate was warmer and wetter than it is now, redwoods grew throughout the northern hemisphere. It is the low-lying coastal fringe of northern California, no more than 30 miles wide and 3,000 feet high, that today most nearly reproduces those conditions. Coast redwoods thrive amid the heavy rains and sudden fogs of this area, growing in dense, cloistered groups; the ground carpeted with needles and moss, the sky almost hidden by the overlapping branches, their tiny leaves a delicate green.

There can be no disputing that these magnificent and awesome trees are the first priority for every visitor to the National Park. But there is much else to observe. Every spring and fall brings migrating birds. On land there are Roosevelt elk, mountain lion and blacktail deer; gray whales, porpoises, seals and sea lions in the ocean; beaver, mink and river otters in the freshwater rivers. The Park is in short a paradise – a paradise that man and nature can share peacefully, where the natural world can thrive and man can be at rest.

ROCKY MOUNTAIN

If any one area can symbolize the great American outdoors, the Rocky Mountain National Park must surely be that place. Within its 263,000 acres are to be found no less than 65 peaks of more than 10,000 feet. And amid this towering splendor – the product of volcanic activity over some 60 million years and then of several great ice ages whose glaciers formed and cut the land to its present shape – there is abundant wildlife, carpets of wild flowers, forests, and cool, high, mountain lakes.

This is a truly fascinating environment, for here there are no less than four distinct climates, each succeeding the other as one climbs higher. At the lowest level, the Plains Zone (4,000 to 6,000 feet), there are relatively few trees, and the characteristic landscape is short grass. The Montane Zone (6,000 to 9,000 feet) supports alders, willows, ponderosa pines and the celebrated Colorado blue spruce, elsewhere a popular ornamental tree. Above this lies the Subalpine Zone (9,000 to 11,500 feet), where the Engelmann spruce grows alongside numerous wild flowers – among them marsh marigolds, primroses and Colorado blue columbines – the state flower. Finally, the Alpine Zone is reached. The trees stop at 11,500 feet – although in sheltered spots a thin line may stretch higher still – giving way to Alpine flowers, grasses, mosses and lichens. The Trail Ridge Road, the highest through road in North America, provides an unparalleled opportunity to study environments normally inaccessible to all but climbers and the hardiest walkers. Beyond the tree line, the marked trails must be followed. The Alpine ecosystem is fragile, and even a short diversion from the path may cause irrecoverable damage.

The best way to explore the Park, and to take in its full majesty, is undoubtedly on foot. There are over 300 miles of trails, and overnight trips (a permit is required) take you into the back country, far from the roads and the developed areas. But even if you choose to do your exploring by car, you will surely be overawed by nature's work.

SEQUOIA AND KINGS CANYON

These two National Parks, administered as one unit, lie in the heart of the Sierra Nevada – the great mountain range that runs for 400 miles, north-west to south-east, through eastern California. The land is the product of a great geological upheaval, in which the earth split along a fault. One block was lifted up and tilted westward over the neighboring land, forming a high mountain range. The resulting steep escarpment on the eastern edge of the Sierra Nevada, where the land rises sheer out of the desert, is a classic and dramatic example of fault-block building.

But, the impact of geological forces was not yet complete. One result of the tilting was that the rivers flowed faster and their cutting force increased. Together with the great glaciers that covered the land, they carved out spectacular canyons; sculpted huge, natural amphitheatres, called cirques, and scooped out basins that later became lakes.

The natural phenomenon for which these two National Parks are justly most celebrated is, however, young by the geological clock, though ancient in human terms. The giant sequoia (the tree is named in honor of the great Cherokee chief) is now found only on the western slopes of the Sierra Nevada, growing in isolated groves above about 5,000 feet. Some 40,000 specimens remain: a substantial number, one might think, until one recalls the depredations of the loggers who, in the last four decades of the 19th century, wantonly destroyed entire forests. The establishment of the National

Park in 1890 put a stop to this vandalism, but not before at least two trees even bigger than the celebrated General Sherman Tree had been lost.

The General Sherman, in Giant Forest on the western side of Sequoia National Park, is one of the largest and most ancient living things on our planet. Some 2,500 years old – it was already a mature tree at the time of Jesus Christ – it stands 272 feet tall, with a trunk 36 feet in diameter. Here, in the beauty and majesty of these National Parks, you may enjoy scenery as stunning as you will find anywhere on the continent and can wonder at these timeless marvels of nature.

SHENANDOAH

Artefacts and burial mounds left by the earliest settlers on the Blue Ridge Mountains have been found. But otherwise, nothing remains now to tell us of what was probably several thousand years of human habitation. More recently, the first European settlement began in the Shenandoah valley in 1716, and in little more than two centuries the land and its plentiful resources were exploited and worn out. Only dedication, determination and vision – a magnificent vision of how the land might be restored to something of its former glory – were able to prevent complete disaster.

Settlement began harmlessly enough, with small numbers of immigrants coming along the Shenandoah River from Pennsylvania and farming the low-lying land. It was in the 19th century, when the lowlands were full and population pressures were increasing, that the damage began. Agriculture moved up the mountains, but winning a living from high ground is hard. Land must be cleared and centuries-old trees felled; wildlife is hunted and destroyed; sheep and cattle are grazed. By the early years of the present century, much of the land had been stripped of its goodness; if not by agriculture then by mining for copper, iron and manganese. The farmers and miners moved on, leaving behind them a blighted landscape and a depressed and poverty-stricken people.

After years of legal wrangling – and many years before that of campaigning by people such as George Freeman Pollock, who owned 5,000 acres of mountain top and the celebrated Skyland Resort – a National Park was established in 1935. The remaining inhabitants were resettled; Skyline Drive along the ridge of the mountains was built, and the stage was set for an almost unique experiment – an attempt to restore an area to its former natural state. Nearly fifty years on, the experiment seems to have worked – and worked better than could perhaps ever have been foreseen. Over 95 per cent of the Park is now forested, and there are some hundred species of tree. And many animals, long since driven from their former home, have now returned: deer, turkey, bear and bobcat among them.

Shenandoah National Park is a true success story, a living witness to the value of the conservation ideal.

THEODORE ROOSEVELT

One does not normally associate those who hold the greatest office in the land – that of President of the United States of America – with the outdoor life. Whatever the circumstances of their upbringing, politicians today and for many decades past, have seemed more at home in the smoke-filled rooms of caucus meetings than under the wide-open skies, where man can sense his insignificant place in the scheme of things.

But it was not thus with Theodore Roosevelt, President from 1901 to 1909. Nearly twenty years before he entered the doors of the White House, he came to the North Dakota Badlands to hunt bison. Even then, the area's 'dismal beauty', as he once described it, must have exerted a strong pull, since before he returned east he had become a partner in the Maltese Cross Ranch. Just a few months later, it proved a literal lifesaver. In February 1884, Roosevelt's wife and mother died on the same day. The young politician retreated west to overcome his grief and recharge his spirits on his Badlands ranch.

Roosevelt spent two and a half years in North Dakota. Although his interest in his ranches (he founded his own, the Elkhorn, while remaining a partner in the Maltese Cross) later diminished, it was at this time that he developed the concern for the environment, and for the proper use of resources, that characterized his presidency. In his White House years, he established the Forest Service, signed the Antiquities Act, proclaimed fifteen sites of historic interest and also set up five national parks. In his many writings, too, Roosevelt did much to promote the conservationist cause.

What was the land that so attracted him? It is typical Badlands scenery: bizarre shapes sculpted by the action of water cutting through soft strata, towering out of a dry land sparsely covered with grass and sagebrush. The land seems unforgiving and unwelcoming, but there is much animal life, including bighorn, bison and antelope, once hunted to near-extinction but now reintroduced by the National Parks Service. Theodore Roosevelt would undoubtedly have approved.

VIRGIN ISLANDS

Tourism and all the trappings of late-20th century 'civilization', are a constant threat to the islands of the Caribbean. The Virgin Islands National Park is a courageous – and successful – attempt to preserve an unspoilt environment and its delicate ecological balance.

The island of St John, the smallest of the three inhabited US Virgin Islands (there are nearly 60 other uninhabited islets), which lie between Puerto Rico and the British Virgin Islands, is the site for the National Park. The Park area covers about three-quarters of the island – and a significant amount of ocean, too. It is in the ocean that the Park's most intriguing and beautiful natural feature is to be found: its coral reefs. The coral fringes the white sand beaches, protecting them from winter waves. It grows from rock outcrops and small rocky cays (islands), in a profusion of endlessly fascinating colors and textures, and is home to many different fish that gleam and glint in the clear, bright waters.

On land, signs of the once-important sugar industry are vanishing rapidly. The sugar plantations were developed by Danish settlers, the first formal white inhabitants, in the late-18th century. Slaves were imported from West Africa to work the land. But in 1848, emancipation brought the great estates to an end, and now the original, subtropical, moist forest is returning. At Leinster Bay, the Annaberg sugar mill and plantation area have been partially restored, and in Reef Bay the ruined estate house and the steam-powered sugar mill can be seen. Elsewhere, on the southern and eastern slopes of the island, there is subtropical dry forest, and on the southern and eastern shore conditions are desert-like, with turks head and dildo cacti.

This is an island for physical rest and mental refreshment: one of the most fortunate benefits of the National Park concept.

VOYAGEURS

The voyageurs (the word is French for travellers) who gave their name to this National Park were a unique group of frontiersmen. Their commodity was fur. Their means of transport was birch-bark canoe. Their strength and character were legendary. And their special knowledge was of the myriad waterways of northwestern North America and of the customs of the indigenous Indian inhabitants.

These men were middlemen in the fur trade – the trade that more than any other established the economic viability of northern North America. Pelts were in demand in Europe – in great demand, and the business was a profitable one. The voyageurs travelled between the Indian trappers of the north-west and the fur-dealers of Montreal, bringing pelts to the one and manufactured items to the other in exchange. It was a tough and dangerous business. Voyageurs would leave Grand Portage and Fort William on Lake Superior in spring, as soon as the ice and snow began to melt, and make for the interior, often travelling for as long as sixteen hours a day. Their exchanges made, they returned south before the autumn snows began. The voyageurs were independent, colorful, resolute men; cheerful and indomitable; prepared to accept great physical discomfort and willing to risk their lives in the pursuit of their trade.

The National Park founded to commemorate them lies along one edge of the Voyageurs Highway, the water route from Lake Superior to Lake of the Woods, on the eastern edge of Ontario Province. It is a watery world. There are literally hundreds of ponds, lakes and streams, gathered in depressions left by the mighty continental glaciers – sheets of ice no less than 2 miles thick – that covered the area within the last million years. Travel is by boat or floatplane, or on skis in winter. Here there are osprey, eagle and great blue heron; cormorants, mergansers, loon and kingfishers. There are timber wolves and coyote. And of course there remain the beavers, still building their ponds as they have for centuries past, their coats, however, no longer here the goal of hunters.

WIND CAVE

Wind Cave National Park takes its name from a curious, natural phenomenon, for which changes in atmospheric pressure are said to be responsible. When the pressure in the open air is greater than that inside the cave, the wind blows into the cave. When it is less outside then in, the wind reverses direction and blows out. It is said that the two local cowboys who discovered the cave in 1881, did so because they heard a strange, whistling sound – the noise of wind escaping through a blowhole.

Inside the cave, there are 1¼ miles of passages and caverns to explore. A further 32 miles have been discovered, but are left in their natural state, and there may well be more: no one knows how far Wind Cave actually does extend. The fascinating and beautiful feature of the cave are the boxwork patterns that cover its limestone walls. These are the result of calcium carbonate, or calcite. The calcite was deposited in countless tiny cracks and crevices in the limestone; the limestone slowly wore away and a fragile network of crystal, shimmering red and pink, was left.

There is also much to see above ground, where the Park is a fascinating example of the original prairie ecosystem. There are many prairie grasses and, in spring and summer, wild flowers. Of the Park's many animals, the bison and the prairie dog are the most interesting. Bison once lived on the prairie in their thousands. Virtually wiped out by the end of the last century, they are now returning, due to the care of conservationists who have built up the stock over many decades. The prairie dog population was similarly depleted. At the turn of the century, there were some 400 million of these swift little rodents. Today, they are virtually extinct, although two towns – as packs of prairie dogs are called – do survive here.

YELLOWSTONE

The Yellowstone National Park is a peaceful land; a huge tract in which wildlife can roam undisturbed, and man is the visitor. There are 3,500 square miles of wilderness – home for bear, elk, bison, moose, antelope and many other mammal and bird species. There are many natural landscape beauties – among these is the Grand Canyon of the Yellowstone, no less than 24 miles long and 1,200 feet deep.

Here are some 10,000 geysers, pots of boiling mud, fumaroles (steam vents) and sulphur springs: the visible, outward sign of seething, liquid rocks buried deep within the earth. Geysers occur because deep underground, liquid rock, or volcanic magma, and a water source meet. The water is heated, and steam and hot water are forced upwards through faults in the rocks. Eventually, the pressure underground becomes so great that steam and water spurt out in gigantic jets. The entire Yellowstone basin is a caldera, a huge bowl created after a mammoth volcanic eruption some 600,000 years ago.

The most celebrated of all the geysers at Yellowstone is 'Old Faithful' – so called because of the frequency of its eruptions, which happen every 64 1/2 minutes on average, although intervals of as little as 30 and as much as 90 minutes, are not uncommon. The waters reach a height of 115 to 150 feet, some 12,000 gallons being expelled in only a few minutes. Here, and at many other geysers in the Park – Mammoth Hot Springs, New Highland Terrace and White Elephant Back Terrace, for instance – beautiful terraces of travertine, often etched in unusual shapes, form a graceful background to the steaming waters. The travertine is a form of calcium carbonate dissolved in the waters that carry it to the surface and left behind after they evaporate.

Here in Yellowstone, there is permanent evidence – evidence one can never forget – that the earth is its own master and is not for taming by man.

YOSEMITE

This was one of the places where the conservationist idea first took root – deservedly so, and not a moment too soon. Deservedly because, of all the beauty and majesty contained in all the national parks scattered across the nation Yosemite represents, at least in the opinion of many, the pinnacle. And not a moment too soon, because a scarce ten years after white men finally expelled the Ahwahneechee Indians from their home, a true tourist trade had already begun to threaten Yosemite's unique splendors.

Thousands of years ago, glacial ice carved the awesome landscape we see today. Glaciers broadened the canyon on the Merced River to form the Yosemite Valley, seven miles long and almost two miles wide, scouring and carving through the joints in the weaker rock, but leaving the harder rocks intact. Pre-eminent among these is the aptly named El Capitan, its sheer walls 3,600 feet high, the largest block of granite on earth. Glaciers also formed the spectacluar waterfalls that drop, unimpeded by intervening ledges, down the sheer canyon walls. The greatest of these is the Upper Yosemite Falls, the highest on the continent. They fall free to a ledge 1,430 feet below and then drop a further 1,000 feet.

If Yosemite ended here, these would be splendors enough. But there is also the Grand Canyon of the Tuolumne River further north, whose walls retained their V-shape despite the force of the glacial ice. There are the sequoia groves, including Mariposa Grove where the Grizzly Giant vies with General Sherman in Sequoia National Park for the title of oldest tree. And there is the fascinating Alpine scenery of Tuolumne Meadows and the high country, with abundant wild flowers and wildlife.

For visitors prepared to leave their cars and take to their feet, Yosemite offers much. A half-mile hike is all that is needed to enter a new world – a world in which man is dwarfed and awed, yet renewed as well.

ZION

Centerpiece of the Zion National Park without question, is the canyon of the Virgin River; an extraordinary tribute to the powerful and persistent force of water. For it is water, seeking a path through the rock, that has created the immense, perpendicular walls of the canyon, half a mile high and normally about a quarter-mile apart. At one point the spectacular Narrows – the gap between the walls – closes to a mere 20 feet, far less than the average city street. One can hardly believe that this normally sluggish water could develop such force and create such amazing works of nature. But three million tons of rock are carried downstream to the confluence with the Colorado every year, and after the summer rains the quiet stream becomes a raging torrent.

What, besides the canyon itself (along which hikes are possible), awaits the visitor in this National Park? There is fishing, horseback-riding and above all, a wide variety of walks and hikes to suit people of all energies. There is also the chance to study the fascinating geology of the area, for the rocks here are a record of changes over many millions of years, and there are fossil records of great reptiles, the first birds and some early mammals. The vegetation repays interest, too. Along the floor of the canyon there is riparian woodland; above the cliffs, woodland and open land dotted with shrubs; and finally high country, with ponderosa pine and Douglas fir. Many species of bird live throughout the year in the Park, but migrate for the winter from the high country down to the canyons.

And the curious name? How did that come about? Joseph Black, a Mormon pioneer who lived on the outer edge of the canyon, named it Zion, which means 'the heavenly city of God'. Brigham Young, the Mormon leader, disagreed. He called it *Not* Zion, but Black's original and more positive description has held sway.

Previous page: **Bass Harbor Lighthouse, Acadia National Park,** on New England's rock-strewn coastline. These pages: **historic New Market Battlefield Park** above **and an elegant colonial-style home** facing page, **set against the snow-clad landscape of Virginia's Shenandoah National Park.**

Winding its tortuous way through the mist-shrouded mountains, Newfound Gap Road *above* **reveals to the visitor some of the splendors of the Great Smoky Mountains National Park.** *Facing page:* **the boulder strewn course of the Little Pigeon River.** *Overleaf* **the Oconaluftee River** *left* **and Grotto Falls** *right.*

Basking in the light of a setting sun, the autumn foliage of
Cades Cove *above* takes on an incandescent, golden color.
Also in Tennessee's Great Smoky Mountain National Park is
the rock-strewn Little River *facing page*.

Florida's steamy Everglades National Park *these pages and overleaf* **is a magical, prehistoric-looking area of dense mangrove swamp and rich subtropical vegetation. It is in these once-threatened surroundings that many endangered species of wildlife now flourish.**

Alligators *above and top*, once widely sought after for their skin, are now protected and are frequently to be seen basking in and beside the shallow waters of the Everglades. *Facing page*: sunset over Everglades National Park.

Washed by the warm, clear waters of the Caribbean, Virgin
Islands National Park is a paradise of unspoilt beaches and
thickly forested mountains, as at Trunk Bay *facing page*.
Above: an idyllic sunet scene at Maho Bay.

Virgin Islands National Park occupies some three quarters of the island of St. John, where picturesque bays, such as Europa Bay *above,* **Cinnamon Bay** *top right* **and Salt Pond Bay** *bottom right,* **are a feature of its magnificent coastline.**

Facing page: **coral reefs in Leinster Bay.**
Overleaf: **the majestic 'Window from the Basin'** *left* **and awesome Santa Elena Canyon** *right,* **one of three huge canyons carved by the Rio Grande in Big Bend National Park.**

BOQUILLAS CANYON

100 MILLION YEARS AGO, WHAT IS NOW KNOWN AS THE BIG BEND COUNTRY WAS COVERED BY A SHALLOW OCEAN. DURING THIS TIME, THOUSANDS OF FEET OF LIMESTONE WERE LAID DOWN ON THAT OCEAN FLOOR. THE RIO GRANDE HAS CARVED ITS WAY THROUGH THESE LIMESTONE BEDS TO FORM BOQUILLAS CANYON. THIS 1/2 MILE TRAIL WILL TAKE YOU INTO THE CANYON.

This page: **the dramatic scenery of Big Bend National Park where the mighty Rio Grande cuts through the Santa Elena Canyon** *top left*, **and rugged mountains rise above the arid plains.**
Facing page: **hardy desert vegetation, such as the spiky, smooth-leaf sotol, adds a touch of green to the rocky terrain around Hunter Peak, Guadalupe Mountains National Park, southwest Texas.**

Hidden beneath the rugged foothills of the Guadalupe Mountains, and millions of years in the making, Carlsbad Caverns National Park is a wonderland of giant underground galleries filled with rock formations of every imaginable shape, color and size.

Transformed into stone by a magic combination of time and the elements, petrified logs lie scattered over the hostile landscape of the Blue Mesa *facing page* **and the Painted Desert** *above,* **in Arizona's Petrified Forest National Park.**

Renowned for its remarkable 12th century Indian cliff
dwellings, Mesa Verde National Park consists of a sandstone
plateau which rises some 2,000 feet above the surrounding
valleys. *Above*: Square Tower House, in Navajo Canyon. *Facing
page*: lightning rends the sky over Mesa Verde National
Park.

Above: the golden orb of the setting sun silhouettes the
mountain peaks and tableland of Mesa Verde National Park,
Colorado. *Facing page*: Cliff Palace, probably the most
famous of all the Pueblo Indian cliff dwellings to be found
in the park.

From the majestic peaks of Hopi Point *above and facing page*
the splendor of the Grand Canyon's South Rim fans out to
meet the horizon.

Seen from Yaki Point *above* and Moran Point *facing page*,
seemingly countless layers of weather-worn, stratified rock
rise up from the Colorado River and the canyon floor.

Sparse, hardy vegetation clings precariously to the scarred, sun-baked land of Grand Canyon National Park, at Mohave Point *above* **and Yaki Point** *facing page*.

Seen from the rim, the awe-inspiring majesty of the Grand Canyon is laid out like a map *facing page*, while from the Canyon floor, as at Lee's Ferry *above*, the massive, wind-carved rock formations that stand silent sentinel over the Colorado are even more impressive.

**Monumental sandstone rock formations, with names as
evocative as the Watchman** *facing page* **and the Sentinel**
above, **seen across the waters of the North Fork of the
Virgin River, form part of Utah's spectacular Zion Canyon,
in Zion National Park.**

Set within some of Southern Utah's most magnificent landscape, Bryce Canyon National Park is a mixture of cool, tree-covered plateau and, below its rim, a barren land of impressively-colored and fantastically-shaped rock formations. *Facing page*: **Paria View.** *Above*: **the soaring spires and walls of Queen's Garden.**

'Red rocks standing like men in a bowl-shaped canyon' **was
the Indians' poetic name for Bryce Canyon. The remarkable
scenes on the Fairyland Trail** *facing page* **show just how apt
this description was.** *Above:* **evening descends on Bryce
Canyon at Paria View.**

Capitol Reef's fame has been limited not by any lack of magnificent scenery but by the fact that it is less accessible than many of the other National Parks. Larger than both Bryce Canyon and Zion combined, this Utah park stretches 72 miles through the south-central part of the state. The park is named for one of its prominent peaks; Capitol Dome. The contorted monoliths and arches, the eroded canyons and bridges along the Waterpocket Fold – these are the true faces of Capitol Reef.
Facing page: the untamed beauty of Capitol Reef, seen though the massive span of Hickman Natural Bridge. *Left*: the graceful sweep of Cassidy Arch.

**Massive rock formations and tiny figures seen in contrast
against the evening sky** *above*, **from Big Spring Canyon
Overlook, Canyonlands National Park, Utah.
The slow process of erosion that has carved Delicate Arch**
facing page, **in Arches National Park, Utah, from a solid
layer of rock into its present shape, continues
imperceptibly to alter its form.**

the east-central part of Arches National Park *these pages* **is the
 ndow Section, where can be seen the massive, buttress-like
 ndstone spans of Double Arch** *above.* **Here too is the famous North
 ndow** *facing page, top left,* **shown with Turret Arch in the
 ckground, and South Window** *center right.* **Other features, elsewhere
 the park, include Devils Garden** *top right;* **The Organ** *bottom right*
 d the sheer walls of South Park Avenue** *bottom left.*

Rocky Mountain National Park, Colorado, is a wildlife sanctuary whose flora and fauna are strictly protected. Among its more commonly seen inhabitants are the ground squirrel *right*, the chipmunk *below* and the industrious beaver *far right. Bottom right and facing page*: the crystal-clear waters of Bear Creek. *Overleaf* the delicate, trembling leaves of the golden aspen spread a rich blanket of colour over the Colorado woodland scene in the fall.

The craggy, snow-dusted ridges of the majestic Rockies are
a sturdy backbone for the highest state in the nation and
with their valleys, lakes, cascades and forests they form

The jewel-like lakes of Colorado, such as Dream Lake *facing page* and Bear Lake *above and overleaf, left,* reflect the majesty of their settings and are a feature of the Rocky Mountains National Park. *Overleaf, right*: the still waters of Beaver Ponds, Hidden Valley.

Razor sharp teeth and an incredible dexterity are
nborn qualities that the beaver makes full use of
n the construction of his lodge, as shown *these
pages* at Beaver Ponds, Hidden Valley.

Famous for its immense redwoods, Sequoia National Park, in California's
Sierra Nevada, is a land of fascinating diversity. The rich forests on the
lower reaches of the granite slopes give way to the rugged high country,
where snow can be seen throughout most of the year. *Facing page*: Columbine
Lake and Lost Canyon. *Above*: Monarch Lakes, Rainbow Mountain and Mineral
Peak. *Overleaf*: the park's newborn plantlife and ancient redwoods.

The meandering Merced River weaves its way through steep-sided Yosemite Valley *facing page*, **where Bridalveil Falls pour their foaming waters, Yosemite National Park.** *Above*: **the jagged peaks of the Sierra Nevada at Junction Ridge in Kings Canyon, Kings Canyon National Park.**

Above: **the forested floor of Upper Yosemite Valley, and the distinctive shape of Half Dome, pictured from Glacier Point, in Yosemite National Park. From Washburn Point can be seen the cascading Nevada (upper) and Vernal (lower) Falls** *facing page.*

The placid surface of aptly-named Mirror Lake *above*, **cradled in glacier-scoured Tenaya Canyon** *facing page*, **echoes the grandeur of Yosemite's mountains.**

Bumpass Hell *facing page*, **within Lassen
Volcanic National Park, is the area's most spectacular
hydrothermal area. Here, numerous boiling mudpots** *above*,
**pools and fumeroles create a fascinating, almost unearthly
scene.**

The smooth, undulating, cinder hills of the Painted Dunes *facing page*, **in Lassen Volcanic Park, support only the hardiest of pines, in contrast to the verdant banks of rushing Hat Creek** *above.*

A still, blue mist *below* heightens the feeling of isolation in Lady Bird Johnson Grove, Redwood National Park. *Facing page*: dense clouds blanket the redwood landscape.

Reflecting the incredible blue of the clear Oregon sky, the waters of Crater Lake *these pages*, **from whose surface rises the cone of Wizard Island** *facing page*, **are the accumulation of thousands of years of snow and rain. The crater itself was formed when the spent shell of volcanic Mount Mazama collapsed under its own weight.**

Plumes of steaming sulfur gas rise from the restless earth at Halemaumau Firepit *above*, **within the Kilauea Caldera, Hawaii Volcanoes National Park.** *Facing page:* **the wrinkled, forbidding surface of a typical lava field on the island of Hawaii.**

The summit of Mauna Kea, the largest of Hawaii Island's five
volcanoes, rises above its mantle of cloud *above*.
Devastation Trail *facing page* is a half mile of boardwalk
that leads through Hawaii Volcanoes, traversing a ghostly,
barren landscape of tree skeletons and black ash.

The rare silversword *above*, which grows for some twenty years and dies once it has produced its purple bloom, is to be found only on the slopes of Haleakala *facing page*, the world's largest dormant volcanic crater, Haleakala National Park, on the island of Maui.

Apart from the Wind Cave itself, one of the main attractions of Wind Cave National Park are the bison herds *above* which roam the western plains of South Dakota undisturbed. *Facing page*: the rugged North Dakota terrain, in Theodore Roosevelt National Park, that appealed so much to the former President.

Badlands National Park *these pages* **lies between the Cheyenne and White Rivers of South Dakota. Established as a Monument in 1939 and given full National Park status in 1978, this unfriendly yet spectacular land is famous for its great fossil resources.**

The jagged, saw-toothed peaks of the mighty Grand Tetons
tower over the twilight waters of Snake River at Oxbow Bend
facing page and an autumnal woodland scene *above*. *Overleaf*:
snow-covered sagebrush flats at Jackson Hole *left* and
Jackson Lake *right*, Grand Teton National Park, Wyoming.

Hot water, bubbling up from deep within the earth carries with it dissolved limestone which precipitates to form the magical calcium carbonate creations such as Minerva Terrace *above*, at Mammoth Hot Springs, Yellowstone National Park. Also within the park are numerous other geothermal springs, geysers and pools, such as the incredibly tinted Morning Glory Pool *facing page*.

The Lower Falls *above* **crash down over 300 feet into the
yawning, mist-laden Grand Canyon of the Yellowstone River.
Rather more modest and graceful are the Upper Falls** *facing
page***, which arch down for over 100 feet.**

In the depth of winter bison, as well as other animals, are
frequently to be seen in Yellowstone's thermal areas, such
as **Midway Geyser Basin** *above* and **Black Sand Basin** *facing
page*, where the higher ground temperatures and a thinner
covering of snow make food easier to find.

Named for its resemblance to the morning glory flower, the beautifully-colored Morning Glory Pool *above*, in Upper Geyser Basin, is one of Yellowstone's many fascinating tourist attractions. *Facing page*: bison at Opalescent Pool in Black Sand Basin.

Sunrise goldens Mount Sinopah, beyond the shores of Two Medicine Lake *above* **and jagged mountains surround St. Mary Lake and Wild Geese Island** *facing page*, **in Glacier National Park, Montana.**

Facing page: **King of the mighty Cascade Range, regal Mount Rainier raises its snow-encrusted peak above the colorful Alpine meadows at Sunrise, Mount Rainier National Park, Washington State.** *Above:* **pine-circled Bench Lake.**

**Seen from the air, the jagged, glacier-strewn peaks of the
Cascade Range** *these pages*, **in North Cascades National Park,
take on a different, even more forbidding aspect.** *Overleaf*:
**Picture Lake lies in the shadow of Mount Chuksan's mighty
bulk.**

Carved by the elements, the remains of a once-mighty tree
above **lies on Rialto Beach, in the scenic wilderness of**
Olympic National Park's Pacific coast, Washington State.
Facing page: **boats skim the sunlit surface of the Hood**
Canal.

Above and overleaf: **peaceful sunset scenes on Big Bend, Hood Canal, Olympic Peninsula.** *Facing page*: **the dense vegetation in the Hall of Mosses, within the rainforest region of Olympic National Park.**